CHANUKAH

A TRUE BOOK
by
Dana Meachen Rau

Children's Press®
A Division of Grolier Publishing

New York London Hong Kong Sydney
Danbury, Connecticut

The Star of David

Reading Consultant
Linda Cornwell
*Coordinator of School Quality
and Professional Improvement
Indiana State Teachers
Association*

*The photo on the cover
shows a dreidel. The photo
on the title page shows a boy
lighting a menorah.*

Visit Children's Press® on the
Internet at:
http://publishing.grolier.com

Library of Congress Cataloging-in-Publication Data

Rau, Dana Meachen, 1971–
   Chanukah / by Dana Meachen Rau.
      p.   cm. — (A true book)
   Includes index.
   ISBN 0-516-21514-0 (lib. bdg.)   0-516-27059-1 (pbk.)
   1. Hanukkah—Juvenile literature. I. Title. II. Series.

BM695.H3 R36 2000
296.4'35—dc21   00–021082

Contents

Candles glow and gifts await during this joyful winter holiday.

A Jewish Holiday

Chanukah is a happy holiday for Jewish people. Chanukah (also spelled Hanukkah) falls in December. Jews celebrate Chanukah on the twenty-fifth day of Kislev. Kislev is the third month of the Hebrew calendar. Chanukah lasts for eight days and nights.

The first Chanukah was held after a small group of Jewish farmers fought against a large army and won. Their battle reminds people about the importance of freedom and courage in Jewish history.

The Jewish farmers, called the Maccabees, won an important battle.

On Chanukah, families gather. Each night of the holiday is a celebration and a chance to remember the great battle for freedom that happened long ago.

A Fierce King

The story of the first Chanukah is recorded in the ancient Book of Maccabees. In the second century B.C., many Jews lived in Judea, which is the modern country of Israel. Judea was ruled by the Syrian Greeks. Their king was Antiochus IV.

Antiochus believed in the Greek religion, which was the worship of many gods. He tried to force the people of Judea to worship the Greek gods, too. But the Jews refused. Their religion

The Temple of Jerusalem was an important meeting place.

recognized one god. In the city of Jerusalem in Judea, they practiced their religion in a beautiful temple. People would travel far to visit and

worship there. The Temple
of Jerusalem was very
important to the Jews.

Antiochus sent his soldiers
to take over the Temple of

Greek soldiers brought destruction
to the city of Jerusalem.

Jerusalem. The soldiers stole all of the valuables. They replaced items important to the Jews with a large statue of the Greek god Zeus.

A marble head of the Greek god Zeus

Many Jewish people would not worship the Greek gods. The soldiers killed them. Some Jews fled from Jerusalem to escape.

Soldiers also traveled the countryside. In a town called Modi'in, near Jerusalem, soldiers forced people to bow down before a statue of Zeus. A priest named Mattathias refused. He and his sons attacked the soldiers and won.

War of the Maccabees

Mattathias and his sons left Modi'in and hid in the hills. More and more people joined them. They decided to fight the Syrians to get back the right to worship they way they wanted. Mattathias's son, Judas, led the group. He was called Judas Maccabeus

The tombs of the Maccabees, in Modi'in, Israel, today

(the Hebrew word for "hammer") and his group was called the Maccabees.

Judas Maccabeus led the fight against the Syrians.

Judas led surprise attacks on the Syrians. Even though the Syrian army had thousands of soldiers, horses, chariots, and even elephants, the Maccabees won many battles. After three years of fighting, by 165 B.C., the Maccabees had driven the soldiers out of Judea.

The Jews could finally take back the Temple. But when the Maccabees arrived in Jerusalem, they found the Temple was a mess. It took them months to

The Temple was made fit for worship and rededicated with prayer and music.

clean it for worship. They smashed the statue of Zeus. They scrubbed the stone walls. They built a new altar.

Finally, the Temple was clean. Jews from all over Judea came to see the rededication of the Temple. They lit the golden candleholders, called menorahs, of the Temple. The worshippers sang and prayed.

The rededication was held on the twenty-fifth day of Kislev. Judah announced that

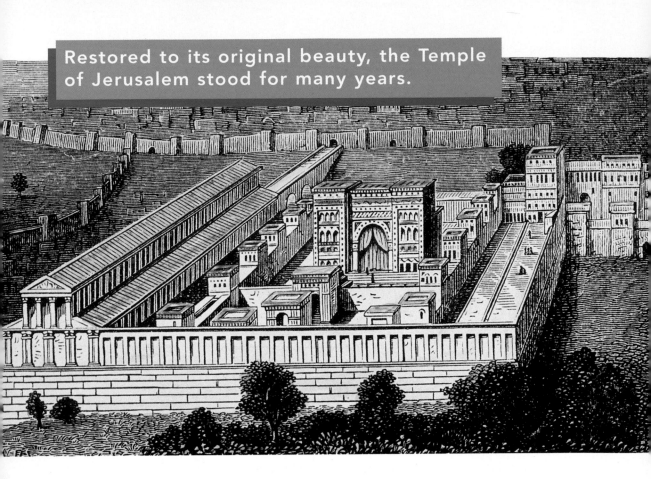

Restored to its original beauty, the Temple of Jerusalem stood for many years.

the rededication of the Temple would be celebrated every year. The holiday was called Chanukah, which means "dedication."

The Miracle

Years later, rabbis (Jewish teachers) created a beautiful legend. They said that during the rededication of the temple, a miracle occurred.

The priests needed to light a special lamp. It held the eternal light—a flame that always needed to burn. The

This eight-wick oil lamp was used in Israel during the 400–500s.

oil for the lamp had to be pure and prepared in a special way. But the soldiers had destroyed most of the jars that held the special oil. Only one small jar was left. It contained just enough to light the flame for one day. It would take another week to prepare more oil, or for someone to bring it from another city.

But then a miracle happened. The oil kept burning. It lasted for eight days!

Miracles

The miracle of the oil has become a favorite part of the Chanukah story for many children.

The oil is not the only miracle of Chanukah. Many people believe that the victory of the small group of Maccabees over the strong and powerful Syrians is also a miracle.

Festival of Lights

Today, just as in ancient times, Chanukah starts on the twenty-fifth day of Kislev and lasts eight days. Chanukah is also called the Festival of Lights. Lighting candles on a menorah, or *chanukiah*, is an important part of the celebration.

Grandfather and grandson light the chanukiah together.

The chanukiah holds eight candles. They represent the eight days of the holiday. The chanukiah also has a place for a ninth candle. It is called the *shammash*, or servant candle, because it is used to light all of the other candles. The chanukiah is often placed in front of a window so it can be seen by people outside.

Families place candles in the chanukiah from right to left, and light them from left to right. A

The shammash, or servant candle, at the upper right, is perhaps the most important candle of all.

A girl recites prayers from the Hebrew prayer book on the last night of Chanukah.

candle is lit on each night of the holiday—one on the first night, two on the second, three on the third, until all eight candles are lit on the last night of Chanukah. Families often pray or sing while the candles are being lit.

Tel Aviv, a city in Israel, is called the City of Lights at this time of year. All of the city lights are left on during the eight nights of Chanukah, and buildings throughout the city display menorahs.

Ways to Celebrate

Besides lighting a chanuki-ah, families follow other traditions on Chanukah. Synagogues hold special services, where choirs may sing traditional music. Jewish schools may present plays or hold special pro-grams or concerts.

At the synagogue, a rabbi lights the menorah.

Reading Chanukah stories together is part of the holiday fun.

Homemade party decorations brighten homes and schools for Chanukah.

At home, families sing, share the story of the Maccabees, or perform traditional dances. People often have Chanukah parties and decorate their

Latkes are fried in oil (above) and served with apple sauce (left).

homes with symbols of Judaism, such as the Star of David. They may serve traditional foods, such as latkes, or potato pancakes. Latkes are made with vegetable oil, which symbolizes the pure oil of the first Chanukah.

Gift giving is also part of Chanukah. Families often exchange gifts on each of the eight nights. One traditional gift is gelt, or money. Families also play games. A common game is played with a four-sided top called a dreidel.

A Dreidel Game

The Hebrew letters Gimmel (left) and Nun (right) can be seen on this wooden dreidel.

On each of the four sides of the dreidel is a Hebrew letter—Nun, Gimmel, Heh, and Shin. These are the initials for the phrase *nes gadol hayah sham*, which means "a great miracle happened there."

To play, each child gets a share of nuts, candy, or coins. There is also a pot of nuts, candy, or coins in the middle. Each child takes a turn spinning the dreidel. If the dreidel lands on Gimmel, the child takes the entire pot. If it lands on Heh, the child takes half. If it lands on Nun, he or she takes nothing. If it lands on Shin, the child has to put part of his or her share into the center.

Freedom and Courage

Chanukah is a joyous holiday. It celebrates the freedom that the Maccabees won. It celebrates the courage of the Jewish people that helped them defeat a strong enemy. It celebrates light during the darkness of winter.

An Orthodox Jew prays by the light of many Chanukah candles.

Traditions are a special part of Chanukah. Menorahs, dreidels, latkes, songs, and games help connect people to the important events that happened more than two thousand years ago. The freedom and courage of the Jews during those events are still important values today.

A public menorah in Washington, D.C.

To Find Out More

Here are some additional resources to help you learn more about Chanukah and other holidays:

Books

Chaikin, Miriam. **Menorahs, Mezuzas, and Other Jewish Symbols.** Clarion Books, 1990.

Corwin, Judith Hoffman. **Hanukkah Crafts.** Franklin Watts, 1996.

Hintz, Martin and Stephen Hintz. **Israel**. Children's Press, 1999.

Stoppleman, Monica. **Jewish.** Children's Press, 1996.

Wood, Angela. **Judaism.** Thomson Learning, 1995.

Organizations and Online Sites

Festivals.com
RSL Interactive
1001 Alaskan Way
Pier 55, Suite 288
Seattle, WA 98101
http://www.festivals.com/

Visit this site to find out about all types of festivals, holidays, and fairs around the world.

The Holiday Page
http://wilstar.com/holidays

Find out about your favorite celebrations at this site, which is devoted to holidays.

Jewish Family
http://www.jewishfamily. com

This online magazine is for the whole family. It includes articles, recipes, art projects, and information about holidays.

Important Words

ancient belonging to a long time ago

courage bravery

eternal to last forever

Hebrew the Jewish language

miracle an amazing event that cannot be explained

rededication the reopening of a building with a special ceremony

symbol an object that stands for something else

synagogue a place where Jewish people meet to pray and worship

tradition a custom, idea, or belief that is handed down from one generation to the next

Index

Meet the Author

Ever since Dana Meachen Rau can remember, she has loved to write. A graduate of Trinity College in Hartford, Connecticut, Dana works as a children's book editor and has authored many books for children, including biographies, nonfiction, early readers, and historical fiction. She has also won awards for her short stories.

When Dana is not writing, she is doing her favorite things— watching movies, eating chocolate, and drawing pictures—with her husband Chris and son Charlie in Farmington, Connecticut.